LONDON
Above Eye Level

W0082459

LONDON
Above Eye Level
Glimpses of the unexpected

John R Murray

Frances Lincoln

© Text and photographs: John R Murray 2007

Designed by John R Murray
(with more than a little help from Octavius Murray)

All rights reserved. No part of this publication may be reproduced,
stored in a retrieval system or transmitted, in any form, or by any
means, electronic, mechanical, photocopying, recording or otherwise,
without either prior permission in writing from the publishers or
a licence permitting restricted copying. In the United Kingdom
such licences are issued by the Copyright Licensing Agency,
Saffron House, 6–10 Kirby Street, London ECIN 8TS.

First published in 2007 by
Frances Lincoln Limited
4 Torriano Mews
Torriano Avenue
London NW5 2RZ
www.franceslincoln.com

ISBN: 978-0-7112-2831-3
Printed and bound in Hong Kong

Contents

Why look up?

This small volume should really be called 'A Passion for Looking Up'. For most of my life I have had fun exploring the world above eye level and I hope that this book will prove infectious.

I can't remember when this passion began. Perhaps an inkling of its approach was revealed when, as a child, I took pity on Little Johnny Head-in-Air in *Struwwelpeter*, that beautifully illustrated yet frightening children's book. I sympathised with Johnny's addiction for looking up and came to his rescue, as he was about to step off the quay, by drawing a long plank over the water to prevent him from falling in. My fascination for looking up was nurtured by an instinctive interest in buildings – their gables, pediments, chimneys, turrets (from which I always imagine princesses letting down their silken tresses to handsome princes below). Shapes and images interested me more than dates and styles.

John Betjeman, in his television programmes, inspired us all to open our eyes and take an interest in buildings and, in particular, to explore the wonders above eye level where so much of the original detail had, and in most cases still has, survived the ravages of the ground-floor shop-front alterations. Many buildings, seemingly rather dull, suddenly take life inhabited by eye-catching detail: from Pont Street Dutch with its terracotta dragons that used to look down from the apex of pediments and, in all too few cases, still do (p.72), to Liberty's in Regent Street with its unusual frieze where the sculptor has sculpted his own audience in case no one looks up from the street below (p.4).

Another person who inspired me to 'look' was Thomas Sharp, author of the classic *Town and Townscape*. He explains: 'It is the kinetic quality of townscape that we are concerned with, as against the more common experience of seeing the town as a series of set "still" views.' He describes this kinetic quality by taking us on a walk with him round Oxford. 'At the northern end of Catte Street, by its junction with New College Lane, the only building to be seen on the west side is the noble cube of the old Bodleian [Library]. Advancing ten yards or so along the pavement, one sees coming into view the first tentative beginnings of the rotunda of the Radcliffe Camera and the upper spire of the University Church. Ten more yards and something like a third of the rotunda and dome and half the church tower are in view. Ten more and the Camera is half out of the angle from the Bodleian and stands free against the surrounding sky – as, in a few yards again, does the tower of the Church beyond. Cube, cylinder, the pure primeval elemental forms are suddenly juxtaposed; or, rather, with a rapidity that is almost suddenness, deploy out from each other in a series of effects that is architecturally sensational; a series of effects that illustrates in very essence, the characteristic quality of the kinetic attribute.'

It is this experience described by Thomas Sharp that makes the hunt for detail so stimulating. Spires telescope down and vanish as you approach the intervening buildings that in their turn rise up the closer you get to them. As you turn a corner, new vistas open up and, as you walk along, architectural gems or intriguing details come and go, now revealed, now hidden, nothing is static. Everything seems to be on the move. Exploring a city in this way is a truly kinetic experience.

It is fascinating to find how much detail can be seen above eye level yet how few people seem to notice it. I once stopped someone in Bond Street and pointed at a glamorous female nude caryatid on one of the buildings (p.107). 'My goodness', she responded, 'I've never noticed her and I have been working here for years.' On another occasion, in Charing Cross Road, I pointed up at the vast chariot and charioteer on what was then the Talk of the Town (p.54). 'Is that new?' I was asked. This was from someone who had worked in the area for fifteen years!

Walking the streets looking up is fraught with danger. To begin with, parking meters are so skilfully designed that if you bump into one while looking up, your chin comes cracking down on top of it. Obviously there is the hazard of colliding with people but usually they get out of your way. Those with dogs are a different matter. Inevitably the owner moves aside to avoid you while the dog, pulling on the retractable lead, decides to take the opposite route. Being trapped in this way can be embarrassing.

Exploring above eye level is a voyage of discovery. You are never quite sure what gem awaits you. Walking down Oxford Street you can, surprisingly, catch sight of a family of beavers cavorting on the gables of No.105 (p.79). This building was put up in 1887 for the hatter, Henry Heath, but the frieze showing the hatter's trade has vanished, only the beavers remain. Up under the eaves of 35 Grosvenor Place (p.26), a 1950s' building looking out over the gardens of Buckingham Palace, you catch sight of what Pevsner describes as 'angels treading down devils'. They look more like a manual of murder techniques. And it is always good to come across detail that relates to the original purpose of a building, such as the RAC Club in Pall Mall (p.14). In the centre of the building is a classical pediment within which there appears, at first sight, to be a normal classical frieze. On closer inspection you notice the putto is driving a motor car – clearly off to rescue Phaeton's chariot! And what about Waterhouse's Natural History Museum (p.60-5) with all those sculptured animals scrambling over it?

My original aim was to photograph detail all over London, but before long I found such riches in the centre that I decided to concentrate on that area. There are, therefore, not many examples of detail outside central London.

This book may become an historical record as already some of the detail I would have liked to include has vanished, for example, the figures that were on the roof and pediments of the Trocadero in Piccadilly Circus. They have been taken down and there is no sign of their return.

Acknowledgements

I have used many reference books and other sources (such as Jane Peyton's enjoyable *Looking Up in London* published by Wiley-Academy) to track down details for the locations and captions. I particularly wish to acknowledge my enormous debt to the new and completely revised London volumes in Pevsner's *The Buildings of England* published by Yale University Press.

Above Eye Level
Photographs

I have placed the captions and the locations at the end of the book for two reasons. First, it is the image that is important and nothing should detract from it. Secondly, the book can be used as a quiz to see how many images you can recognize and place, before checking at the back.

3

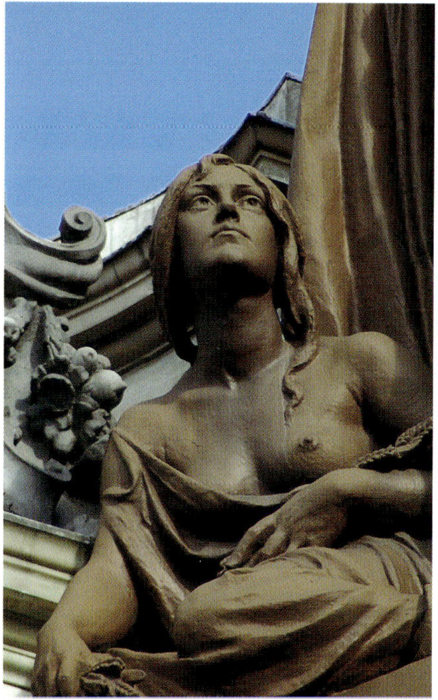

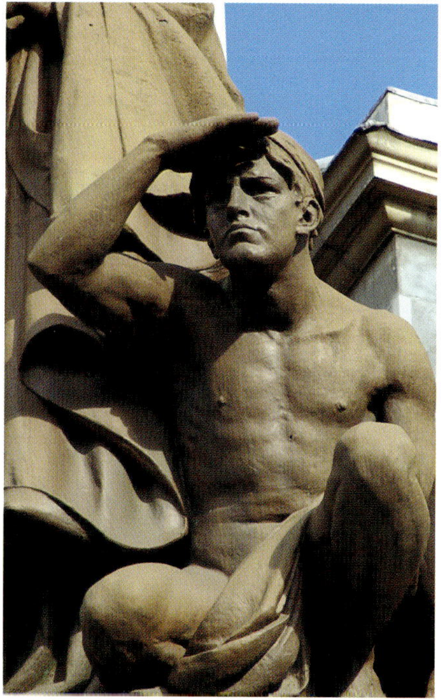

18

24

LOCKE

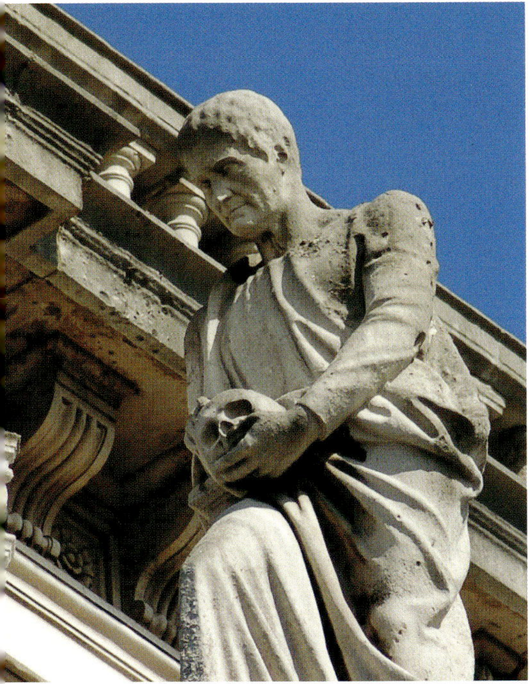

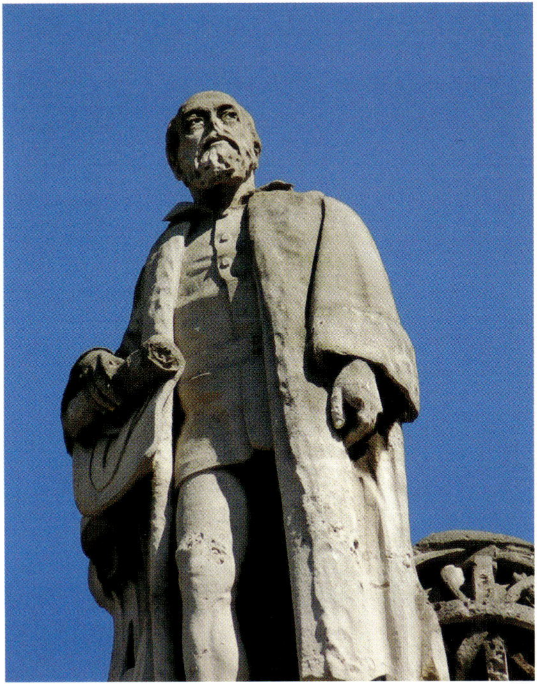

40

41

48

49

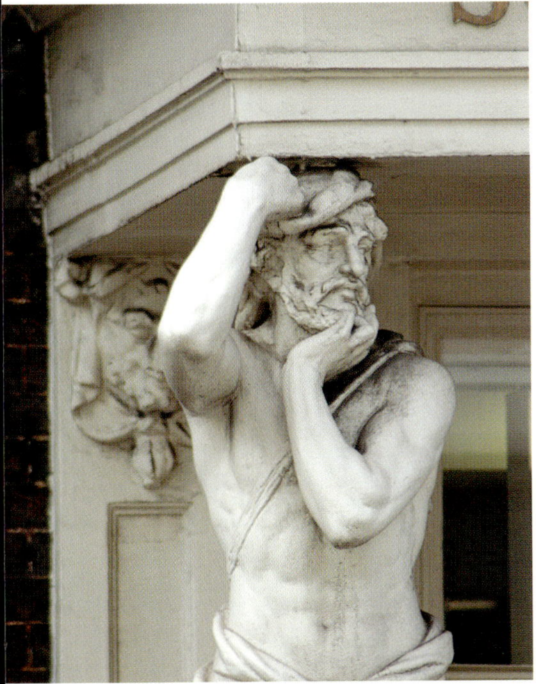

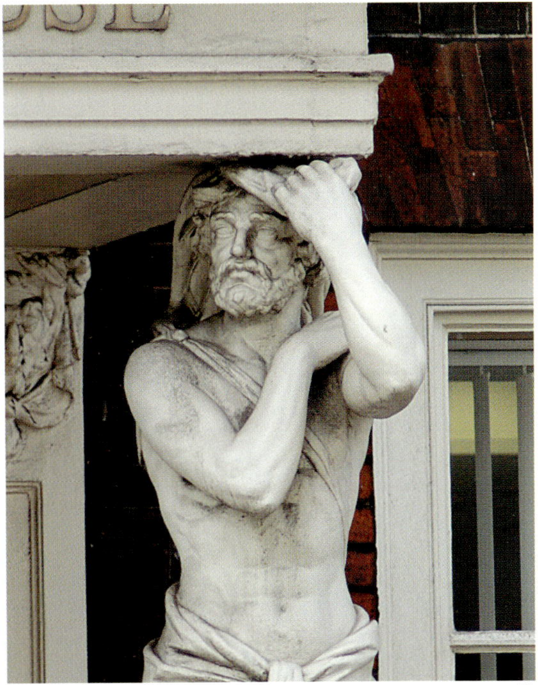

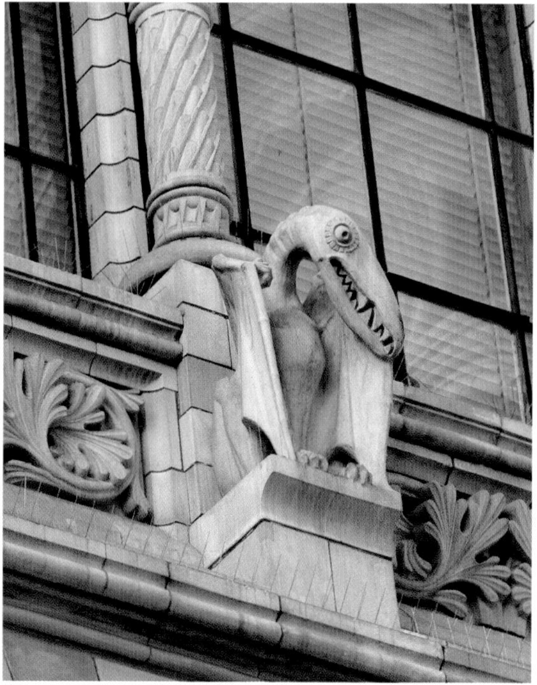

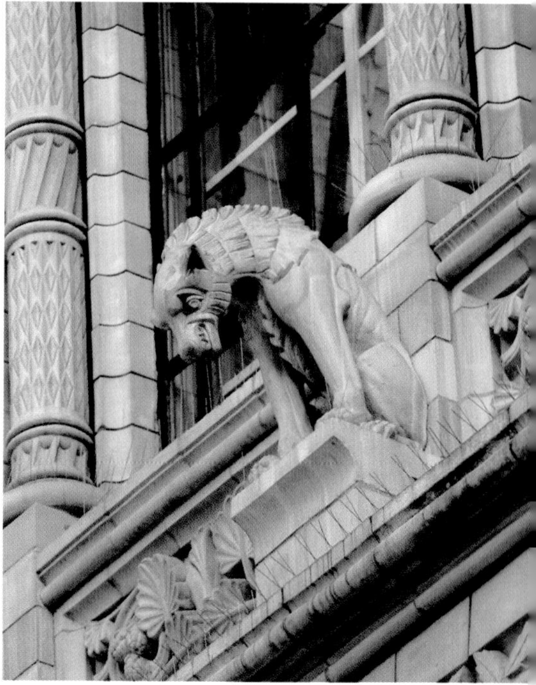

ARCADE

103

ANNO · ELIZABETHAE · R · XIII · CONDITVM · ANNO · VICTORIAE · R · VIII · RESTAVRATVM

122

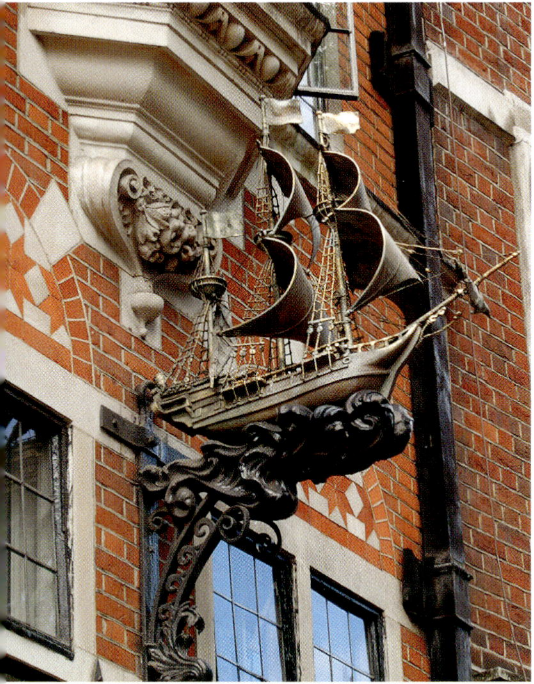

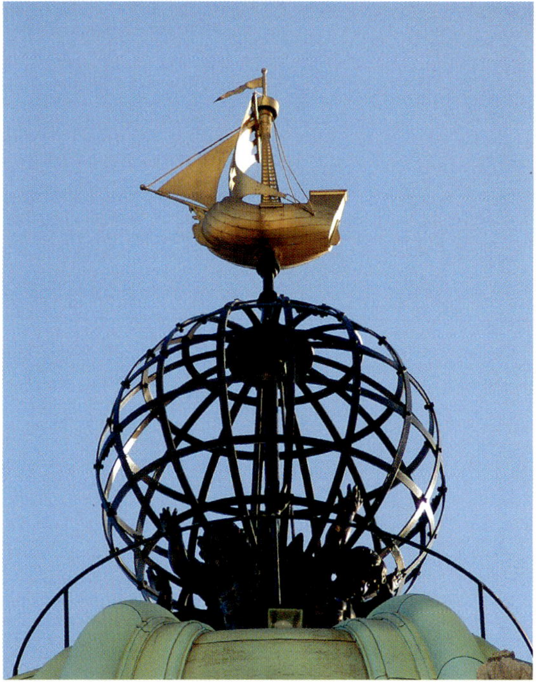

THE
ROYAL
WATERLOO HOSPITAL FOR CHILDREN AND WOMEN

SUPPORTED BY
VOLUNTARY CONTRIBUTIONS

SCALES WEIGHTS
&
WEIGHING MACHINES.

319   321

27

130

Above Eye Level

Captions and locations

Unless otherwise specified, the main details refer to the buildings on which the images appear. In some instances details are missing where I have been unable to identify the sculptor, artist or architect.

Front cover Smithfield Market dragon. West Smithfield EC1. The market building designed by Sir Horace Jones, who was also responsible for Billingsgate and Leadenhall markets, was opened in 1868.

Opposite title page Pterodactyl by Dujardin of Farmer & Brindley. Natural History Museum, Cromwell Road, SW7 (see pp.60–65).

3 Caryatids as mullions. 44 Hallam Street W1, by Eustace Frere, 1915–22, for the General Medical Council.

4–7 Frieze with sculptured audience overlooking the parapet. Liberty's of Regent Street W1, by E.T. & E.S. Hall, 1925–6. Frieze centre modelled by C. L. J. Doman, ends by Thomas Clapperton. Arthur Liberty began to sell oriental silks and Japonnaiserie in 1870. The frieze represents the import of oriental goods into England.

8–9 Golden synchronised divers (some call them the Three Graces) by Rudy Weller. Building on corner of Piccadilly Circus and Haymarket SW1, by Peter Howard of Renton Howard Wood Levin Partnership, 1989–91.

10–13 Coliseum Theatre. St Martin's Lane WC2, by Frank Matcham, 1902–4. Built to rival the Hippodome, Charing Cross Road. Terracotta façade by Hathern of Leicestershire.

14–15 RAC pediment sculpted by Ferdinand Faivre with a putto driving an early motor car. Royal Automobile Club, Pall Mall SW1, by Charles Mewès & Arthur J. Davis, 1908–11.

16–17 Statue of Justice with attendants by H.C. Binney. Corner of Piccadilly and east side of St James's Street SW1, by Ernest Runz & G.M. Ford, 1906–8. Originally for Norwich Union.

18–19 Figurative roundels. 1 Albemarle Street W1 [formerly Albemarle Hotel], by George & Peto, 1887–8.

20–21 Britannia and lion by Hermon Cawthra. Originally County Fire Office, north side of Piccadilly Circus W1, by Ernest Newton 1924–7.

22–23 North Italian gothic. 20 Irving Street, Leicester Square WC2, by A. Wilson, Son & Aldwinckle, 1875.

24–25 Reliefs of 'Sight' and 'Sound' by Bainbridge Copnall. Warner West End, Cranbourn Street, Leicester Square WC2, by E.A. Stone & T. R. Somerford, 1938, in modernist style.

26–29 'Angels treading down devils' (or a manual of murder techniques!) by Maurice Lambert. 25–35 Grosvenor Place SW1, by Wimperis, Simpson & Fyffe, 1956–8.

30–33 88 Burlington Gardens W1, by Sir James Pennethorne, 1867–70. Originally the University of London headquarters and later the Museum of Mankind, now moved to the British Museum. **30–31**

Seated figures from left to right: Newton, Bentham, Milton and Harvey by J. Durham, 1869. **Standing in the background on pediment:** Galileo and Goethe by E. W. Wyon 1869. **32** *(left)* Harvey by J. Durham, 1869; *(right)* Locke in niche by W. Theed, 1869. **33** *(left)* Galen by J. S. Westmacott, 1866; *(right)* Galileo by E.W. Wyon, 1869.

34–35 Two seated figures by L. E. Roselieb. 6 St George Street W1, by C. H. Worley, 1904–5.

36–37 Young musicians by Gilbert Bayes. 17 Cavendish Square (Wigmore Street side) W1, by Henry Keene, 1756 – altered in 1925. This twentieth-century relief was made when the house was Brinsmead's piano showrooms.

38–39 Child sculptors in Coade stone relief, 1796. 25–36 Belgrave Square SW1. Installed here in 1968. Brought from the former Danish-Norwegian consulate in Wellclose Square, Stepney.

40 Prospero and Ariel (from *The Tempest*) by Eric Gill. Broadcasting House, Langham Place W1, by G. Val Myers, 1931. When unveiled this group caused controversy. They were said to be 'objectionable to public morals and decency'. 'Maidens are said to blush and youths to pass disparaging remarks' when viewing it.

41 Panel by Eric Gill. Broadcasting House (see p.40).

42–43 Elaborate sculptured pediment. Cumberland Terrace, Regent's Park NW1. Planned by John Nash 1811, executed by James Thomson, 1826.

44–45 Mythical figures riding hippocamps (half horse, half fish) by W. Theed. Somerset House, Lancaster Place front WC2, by James Pennethorne, 1851–6.

46–47 Circular tower, parish church of St Mary. Angel caryatids probably by J. F. C Rossi. 17 Marylebone Road NW1, by Thomas Hardwicke, 1813–17.

48 *(left)* **Apex figurehead**. 14 Cockspur Street SW1, by A.T. Boulton, 1906–8, for Hamburg-Amerika Shipping Line. *(centre)* **Male head with profile carved below**. Burlington Arcade entrance, 51 Piccadilly W1. Sculptor Benjamin Clemens. *(right)* **Palace Theatre** detail. Cambridge Circus WC2, built for Richard D'Oyly Carte. Designed in pink terracotta by G.H. Holloway & T.E. Collcutt, 1888–91.

49 *(top left)* **Crouching female figure** by Farmer & Brindley after L. J. Chavalliaud. 31 Old Bond Street W1, by Beresford Pite, 1898–1900. *(bottom left)* **Torch-bearing lady**. The old Electric Cinema, 1908–9, converted from a shop, Upper Street, Islington N1. *(right)* **Detail from group of figures** by Harold Parker. One group on each side of the corner entrance, Australia House, Aldwych WC2, by A. M & A. G. R. Mackenzie, 1913–18.

50–51 Porch with atlantes of Coade stone (added 1791). Schomberg House, 82 Pall Mall SW1, 1698. Built for the 3rd Duke of Schomberg.

52 *(top left)* **Putto over door** by Gilbert Seale. 70 Jermyn Street sw1, by Reginald Morphew, 1903. *(bottom left)* **Putti holding up the cornice** by Bertram Mackennal. Corner of Piccadilly and west side of St James's Street sw1, by John Belcher jun. & J. J. Joass, 1906–8. Former Royal Insurance Building. *(right)* **Detail with two putti and mythical beasts below**. 26a Conduit Street w1, by A.H. Kersey, 1896–7.

53 *(left)* **Façade detail**. Burlington House, Piccadilly front, Piccadilly w1, by Thomas Banks & E.M. Barry, 1868–73. *(top right)* **Oval bacchic relief**. Brooks's Club, St James's Street sw1, by Henry Holland, 1776–8. *(bottom right)* **Steamship with putti**. Denmark House, 15 Tooley Street se1, by S. D. Adshead for Bennett Steamship Company, 1908.

54–55 Charioteer. London Hippodrome [later the Talk of the Town]. Charing Cross Road wc2, by Frank Matcham, 1898–1900 .

56–59 Britannia presiding over African workers and animals by Benjamin Clemens. Africa House, 64–78 Kingsway wc2, by Trehearne & Norman, 1921–2.

60–65 Guardians of the museum. The ornament and animals are by Dujardin of Farmer & Brindley. The Natural History Museum, Cromwell Road sw7, by Alfred Waterhouse, in the Romanesque style, faced with terracotta, 1872 onwards.

66–67 Eagles in urban eyrie. 22 Old Bond Street w1, c.1905. Renaissance façade of Doulton faience and granite with eagles sculpted in full relief.

68–69 Foliage with birds by John Daymond. (A nest with chicks can be see in the background of the right-hand photograph). 86 St James's Street sw1, by J.T. Knowles jun., 1862–65.

70–71 Dragons. Leadenhall Market EC3, by Horace Jones, 1880–1.

72–73 Gryphon-like beasts. Pont Street SW1.

74–75 Dragon balcony. 5 St George Street W1, eighteenth century.

76–77 Lions surveying Mayfair and St James's. Ritz Hotel, Piccadilly SW1, by Charles Mewès & Arthur J. Davis, 1903–6.

78–79 Terracotta beavers on gables by Benjamin Cresswick. 105–9 Oxford Street W1. Built for Henry Heath the Hatter by Christopher & White, 1887–8.

80–83 Shark, tiger, elephant and ape over door by Barry Baldwin. Allington House, 150 Victoria Street SW1, by Sidell Gibson Partnership, 1997.

84 *(left)* **Winged lion doorway** by Eric Aumonier.

Willing House [now Travelodge], 150 Gray's Inn Road WC1, by Hart & Waterhouse, 1910. *(right)* **Lion**, one on each side of the door, 57 Jermyn Street SW1.

85 *(left)* **Tiger/lion on Asoka column**. India House (see p.86). *(centre top)* **Lion head**. 44 Hallam Street W1. *(top right)* **Bronzework lion** by George Alexander, New Gallery, 115 Regents Street W1 (see p.129). *(bottom right)* **Crouching lion**. 2 Temple Place, Embankment WC2. *(bottom left)* **Roaring lion**. Eversholt Street NW1.

86–87 Elephant balcony. India House, Aldwych WC2, by Herbert Baker & Scott, 1928–30, displaying Indian motifs carved by Charles Wheeler.

88–89 Lion and unicorn (ten feet high) by Tim Crawley. Installed on the tower as part of the 2006 restoration programme to replace the long missing originals. St George's Church, Bloomsbury WC1, by Nicholas Hawksmoor, 1716–31.

Captions and locations

90–91 *(90 left)* **Dogfish**. 16 Waterloo Place SW1, by William Emerson, 1902–6. *(90 bottom)* **Ram** and *(91 top)* **Eagle**, both on the Strand Palace Hotel, Strand WC2, by F. J. Wills, 1928–30. *(90 top)* **Horse's head motif**. The Nag's Head, Floral Street, Covent Garden WC2, by P. E. Pilditch, 1900. *(91 right)* **Dragon holding weathervane**. Spice of Life pub, Cambridge Circus WC2, by Horace M. Wakley, 1899. *(91 bottom)* **Boar's head**. 33 Eastcheap EC3, by R. L. Roumieu, 1868. On the site of the old Boar's Head tavern.

92–93 **Frankenstein monsters**. Regents Palace Hotel, Glasshouse Street W1, by Henry Tanner & W. J. Ancell, 1912–15.

94 *(left)* **Golden Girl** by Michael Rizzello, 1997. On the Plaza [Bourne & Hollingsworth until 1997] Oxford Street W1, by Slater & Moberly, 1925–7. *(top right)* **Atlas figure bracket**. Liberty's neo-Tudor building, Great Marlborough Street W1, by E.T & E.S Hall, 1924. The building timber came from the decommissioned nineteenth-century Royal Navy ships HMS Impregnable and HMS Hindustan. *(bottom right)* **Lady with cow**. 101–104 Piccadilly W1, by Col. R.W. Edis, 1890–2. Originally the Junior Constitutional Club. Said to be the first marble-faced building in London.

95 *(top right)* **Jester corbel**. 12 James Street, Covent Garden WC2. *(bottom right)* **Corbel with figurehead**. Liberty's, Great Marlborough Street W1. *(top left)* **Lady reading**. Ryder Street corner with Bury Street SW1, by G. D. Martin, 1897–8. Originally the Marlborough Hotel. *(bottom left)* **Young atlas**. Pedimented gable with green brick. 137 Piccadilly W1 [now the Hard Rock Cafe] by Thomas Edward Collcut & Stanley Hamp, 1905.

96–97 **Pediment with hop harvesting scenes**. Hop Exchange [now Central Buildings], 99 Southwark Street sE1 by R. H. Moore, 1866. Top floors demolished after a fire in 1920.

98–99 Columns with figures by James Woodford. Standing outside the Royal Institute of British Architects, 66 Portland Place w1, by Grey Wornum, 1932–4.

100–101 Florentine gothic with balcony resting on atlantes brackets and dragons on rail corners. Holborn Viaduct building EC1, by William Haywood and Thomas Blashell, 1863–9.

102–103 Burlington Arcade entrance. Sculpture by Benjamin Clemens. 51 Piccadilly w1. Entrance to the arcade by Beresford Pite: the triple arcade above, 1911, and the Baroque arch with archaic Greek busts together with the coloured mosaics, 1931.

104–105 Royal Arcade entrance. 12 Albemarle Street w1, by Archer & Green, 1879–80.

106–107 Sensuous nude caryatids. 44 Old Bond Street w1, by W. & E. Hunt, 1906.

108 Seated King probably by Richard Garbe. Kingsgate House, 115 High Holborn WC1, c.1900, by Arthur Keen.

109 Lady meditating. New Gallery, 115 Regent Street w1, by John Burnet & Wilson Tait, 1920–5.

110 Angels by T. Simpson. Apollo Theatre, Shaftesbury Avenue, w1, by Lewen Sharp, 1900–1.

111 Hercules taming the horses of Diomedes on pediment by W. Theed. The Royal Mews, Buckingham Palace Road sw1.

112–113 Four muses (goddesses of music, poetry, the arts and science). 11 St James's Square sw1, refronted by Robert Adam, 1774–6. Restored in 1988–91, re-instating Adam features from his drawings and installing the statues on top of the façade.

114–115 Pediment showing Commerce holding the Exchange Charter with merchants and stevedores. Figures by Richard Westmacott jun. Royal Exchange, Threadneedle Street/Cornhill EC2, by Sir William Tite, 1841–4.

116–117 Early Epstein stone sculptures. British Medical Association [now Zimbabwe House], 429 Strand WC2, by Charles Holden, 1907–8. These sculptures by Jacob Epstein have suffered from 'puritanical outcry'. The figures were sculpted in 1907, each cut from a single piece of Portland stone. Holden's design gave them no protection from the elements. Once in situ, they eroded badly. When they were put up there was an uproar from the National Vigilance Association, and from the Press, who claimed that nudes were 'for galleries not public places where young women and servants could see them'. When the building became Southern Rhodesia House the new owners did their best to deface them as 'inappropriate'. Both this and erosion have left them in the state we now see.

118–119 Old public baths. Dunbridge Street E2.

120 Scaly fish decorate the roof and one acts as a weathervane. Old Billingsgate Market, Lower Thames Street, EC3, by Sir Horace Jones, 1874–8.

121 *(left)* **Beaver weathervane**. 60–64 Bishopsgate EC2. Former home of the Hudson Bay Company by Mewès & Davis, 1926–8. The beaver represents the trade in pelts that made their fortune in their early days. *(middle)* **Gilded dragon** made by Robert Bird in 1679 on Wren's spectacular spire. The first true spire to be built after the Great Fire. St Mary-le-Bow, Cheapside EC2. *(right)* **Gilded grasshopper**. Sir Thomas Gresham's device as a weathervane on The Royal Exchange, Threadneedle Street EC2.

22 *(left)* **Galleon weathervane**. 2 Temple Place, Embankment WC2. *(middle)* **Lamp standard with galleon** by Sir Thomas Brock, 1908. The Mall SW1. *(right)* **Galleon weathervane**. On Liberty's building, Great Marlborough Street W1.

23 *(left)* **Galleon** on Swaziland High Commission, 21 Buckingham Gate SW3. *(right)* **Globe with ship weathervane**. 125 Pall Mall SW1, by Smee & Houchin, 1912–3.

24 W.H. & H. Le May, Hop Factors. Borough High Street, Southwark SE1. Southwark was the centre of the hop trade.

25 Wisden's erstwhile home. Transad House, 21 Cranbourn Street WC2. Originally occupied by the publishers of *Wisden Cricketers' Almanack*.

26 Former Royal Waterloo Hospital for Children and Women. Waterloo Road SE1. Originally a dispensary for children in the City, moved to this site in 1812. Rebuilt in 1903–5 by M. S. Nicholson in Lombardic Renaissance style with three tiers of terracotta loggias. Now a university building.

27 Scales, weights and weighing machines. A traditional way of announcing one's trade. 319–321 Grays Inn Road WC1.

28 The setting sun. 179 New Bond Street W1, c.1800. The top storey's 'armorial head-dress' was added c.1897 by Edmund Wimperis & Hubert East for the court photographer, Lafayette.

29 Dome with figures by William Reed Dick. New Gallery, 115 Regent Street W1, by John Burnet & Wilson Tait, 1920–5.

30 Camel train and driver. Peek House, 20 Eastcheap EC3. Originally the London offices of tea and coffee merchants Peek Bros.

An unexpected sight when looking up, during a walk along the river Lee in the East End of London.

John R Murray was, until 2002, a publisher. He has compiled and edited two slim volumes: *A Gentleman Publisher's Commonplace Book* and *Old Chestnuts Warmed Up* (his own personal collection of poetry, verse and doggerel). All his life he has had a passion for looking up and hopes that this book will prove infectious. He has swum the Bosphorus from Europe to Asia, climbed Mount Parnassus by night and has walked from London to Oxford in the footsteps of John Buchan – all with his eyes open! He is by nature restless and inquisitive.